HORRIBLE DANCE

HORRIBLE DANCE
AVERY LAKE

BRICK BOOKS

Library and Archives Canada Cataloguing in Publication

Title: Horrible dance / Avery Lake.
Names: Lake, Avery, author.
Description: Poems.
Identifiers: Canadiana (print) 20210320443 | Canadiana (ebook) 20210325674 | ISBN 9781771315753 (softcover) | ISBN 9781771315760 (HTML) | ISBN 9781771315777 (PDF)
Classification: LCC PS8623.A4195 H63 2022 | DDC C811/.6—dc23

We acknowledge the Canada Council for the Arts, the Government of Canada through the Canada Book Fund, and the Ontario Arts Council for their support of our publishing program.

Canada Council   Conseil des arts
for the Arts   du Canada

ONTARIO ARTS COUNCIL
CONSEIL DES ARTS DE L'ONTARIO
an Ontario government agency
un organisme du gouvernement de l'Ontario

Government   Gouvernement
of Canada   du Canada

Edited by River Halen Guri.
Design by Emma Allain.
The book is set in Arno Pro and Orpheus Pro.

Author photo by Lily Alexandre.

Printed and bound by Coach House Printing.

487 King St. W.
Kingston, ON
K7L 2X7
www.brickbooks.ca

Though much of the work of Brick Books takes place on the ancestral lands of the Anishinaabeg, Haudenosaunee, Huron-Wendat, and Mississaugas of the Credit peoples, our editors, authors, and readers from many backgrounds are situated from coast to coast to coast in Canada on the traditional and unceded territories of over six hundred nations who have cared for Turtle Island from time immemorial. While living and working on these lands, we are committed to hearing and returning the rightful imaginative space to the poetries, songs, and stories that have been untold, under-told, wrongly told, and suppressed through colonization.

For Alec

CONTENTS

Act I: The Home

Act II: The Other

Act III: The Relations of Production

Act I: The Home

Outdoor Cat

There's a nameless sense of –

being at peace

that comes & goes like an outdoor cat.

Sometimes you don't see it for weeks & worry it's dead.

Sometime it's in & out & in & out all day –

hellish & dizzying.

You love it – it's not yours to name.

It's warm, & kind to you –

but it belongs to the birds it kills.

Pre-Transition House Party Disaster

Bedroom

That's where the blood was happening.

One woman had a knife & one woman had a body.

In, *yank*, out.

In, *yank*, out.

In-ground Pool

My guts invited the water in.

Teens with solo cups watched me sink. One guy wore a suit.

I opened my mouth to smile

& my teeth floated out.

Bathroom

I washed my face in cold water.

I scrubbed my hands raw.

I cornered my head into the sink & thought about growing old as a man.

It was either lipstick, or blood, & I couldn't get it out of my shirt.

Basement

These NDG houses all look the same.

She said her dad was at a hockey game so we could smoke in her basement.

We found a freezer full of butter,

like, fuckin completely full of butter.

Making out with straight girls was this rickety mix of desire & guilt & fear
& obligation & shame.

In each possible world, one of us was a predator.

Back Porch Expanding

Dylan dropped Sarah's pipe & it broke.

I stole beers from some guy's two-four.

Justin Fogel said something about how much vodka I poured.

Sarah agreed with me: everyone's a little bit bi, right?

Zach told everyone he'd shaved his balls.

Ryan didn't wanna finish his forty so I chugged it.

I curled into the sinkholes of a teenage gender.

I dumped the mickey of Jack Daniels in apple juice.

I lay down in the middle of the road,

calling it a suicide attempt,

but these were suburban fucking house parties.

Cedar Drive didn't have the traffic to kill me.

I gave so many fake names to guys who played rugby.

I said I was called Timothée Chalamet (no relation).

We pulled pranks like hiding butter all over the house.

I drank most of Seb's beer.

My rictus got wider.

If some dude left his solo cup unattended I'd steal it.

I saw the knife coming & forced a smile.

I told my ex I was trans while blackout drunk.

What happened was I noticed they were at the party & instantly drank
most of a bottle of whiskey like muscle memory.

I put "In the Air Tonight" on the speakers so I could watch bros anticipate
the drum bit,

alone in the malevolent knowledge that there's a full three minutes before
the drum bit actually hits.

I put on music my ex liked.

This went on for like four years.

I drank everything Courtney brought.

I went to Halloween parties as "a girl."

Someone threw a painting through a window.

Someone handed me a garbage bag to puke in. I missed.

Someone kneed me in the stomach.

Someone brought fucking Baileys.

Someone had been using the bathroom for half an hour.

Someone thought I stole their jacket.

Someone asked if I was alright.

Someone said my shirt made me look like I was in Odd Future.

Someone said "Oh shit, from behind I actually thought you were a girl."

I puked in the metro.

I'm pretty sure I never cried.

I sunk to the bottom.

I did really fucking good in school.

I lay still as she ran the knife into me again.

I was certain only that I deserved it.

I watched the sedans & the trees, looming & angular from down on
the asphalt.

Parts of Men's Bodies That Tell Their Confessions and Horrors

A name is a knife.

Man #38

Fingers wheel the pen, until it leaves.

Lonely hands: so many sad potentials when she leaves.

Man #613

Apartment without food, but flush with art and skin.

And then the art leaves.

Man #8

Along the calf, a ruddy scar. Years ago, an ankle met a skate.

Voice forced quiet with swollen gasping fear. Of course it never leaves.

Man #557

Serratus anterior: the boxer's muscle. Hard, tight, knotted: a tree remembers

who it hurts. Beneath the armpit, muscle red and dry as autumn leaves.

Man #21

Skin-scraped hunger. He prays in aching blasts of wither.

Binding body punctured, seeping. Soon, again, she leaves.

Man #80

Practiced cigarettes. Hug like plywood.

Also practiced: early, fast, he leaves.

Man #14

Saws arranged in order, as if they could sing. Chalky skin as he was carried out.

He was quiet and died quietly. Back porch he built reclining, roof collecting leaves.

On Womanhood

1.

I dreamed of a self more porous *Oh, you've got a*
new one now?
I was eighteen, nineteen, miserable

Watching gender rise like a sun, *Oh, you've got a*
new one now? spread like spilled paint

Grey city stained with an inevitable *Oh, you've got a*
new one now? woman

Does she know how quick you change your mind?

I dreamed of a self more porous **Oh, you've got a new one now?**
I was eighteen, nineteen, miserable

Watching gender rise like a sun, **Oh, you've got a new one now?** *spread like spilled paint*

Grey city stained with an inevitable **Oh, you've got a new one now?** *woman*

Does she know how quick you change your mind?

2.

You change your gender & suddenly everyone's a critic. My womanhood
is a cipher for the gender of others. My father said he'd failed as a father, as
a man – I degendered him. Yours too, eh? Hey – can I get you some water?
How many tenderqueer chasers begged me to fuck them, to fill them with
transsexualism via cum? Not hungry for my cock, per se, but for the future
they'd read in it – *this vein here means there's a new gender waiting for me in
the wings*. Easier to get girldick than look their want in the face. You know
the type – churns through early-transition tgirls like hot chips – "I get
older, they stay the same age" if McConaughey's haircut was worse. People
see my gender & think, *I gotta get in on this somehow*. And they say we don't
have to deal with the speculum! Har har har. And the TERFs – desperate
to prop up a flailing, failing womanhood against us. Why so insecure,
babes? You hear Janice Raymond probably got her girlfriend stolen by
Sandy Stone back in the day? Paints the Empire affair in a different light,
doesn't it. Well, this was a fun chat! Take care, stay safe, love you. Text me
when you get home, yeah?

3.

Open Letter to TERF Profs:

Do you ever notice
how on gusty fall days
the leaves skitter across the road all grouped together

It probably won't be long before we both die
Let's take bets
You: heart disease, late seventies, rich and alone
Me: suicide, mid thirties, nestled gently between the road and the tread of
the truck tires

And what happens then, after we're dead, do you think
No, really, I want to know what you think
If maybe you think it's something nice

I don't care if you see the small beauty
I don't care what you think about leaves or angels

I can't bring myself to really hate you
But I don't need to
History's coming
I won't blink first

4.

"She pays the debt of life not by what she does but by what she suffers—
by the pains of child-bearing, care for the child, and by subjection to
man, to whom she should be a patient and cheerful companion.

[...]

That woman is by nature intended to obey is shown by the fact that
every woman who is placed in the unnatural position of absolute inde-
pendence at once attaches herself to some kind of man, by whom she is
controlled and governed; this is because she requires a master."

—Arthur Schopenhauer

5.

It's at least a bit tempting to eroticize "this is because she requires a
master," right?

6.

On April 28, 2021, I tweeted:

> "if i were the type i could write a little essay about how the whole mtftm
> thing has to do with how trans women are a priori barred access to 'non-
> binary' as a category, and the desire to have our transness perceived as eileen
> myles-style radical intervention rather than the regressive, gross chore
> transfemininity is framed as by transmisogynists (read: everyone) –– but
> instead ill just make my little posts and call it a day. does this also have a lot to
> do with my (largely miserable) early 20s spent fucking (largely transmisogy-
> nist) tenderqueers? well what do you think."

It got a bunch of retweets and it made me go on private for a while cuz having a correct post about transmisogyny go viral is an easy way to have a horrible time on twitter.

So, the chasers – in the end, I wanted their gender too. A chic vision of "non-binary" – dashing in epaulets, innovative & sleek as a tech startup. Cuz when I do it, of course, I get the """"they/them"""" with a big wink to the camera – or, more often, they just go full Weather Girls & rain "he's" like confetti. To be transfem, but butch, or god forbid nonbinary, reads as Serano's image of the pathetic failed transsexual – raw & hairy not as sedition, or intention, but abjection. *Oh, he – sorry, she – sorry they – hasn't learned how to shave yet, poor thing.* I wanted to prove I could reach the knife's-edge femininity demanded of me, loop back around, get read as transmasc, and finally be seen as breaking new gendered ground – & not a sad man giving up halfway to womanhood.

It took reading *Stone Butch Blues* to break out of this. There was a lot of me in Jess – more than in the angular asepsis I was chasing. (Chasing! Ha!) Turns out Feinberg was onto something – go figure! Go figure.

7.

You thought of yourself as something
Beautiful that'd shatter on touch
Teacup, white rose

8.

I am a woman [smiles cryptically]

9.

Pain from the angle of redemption
Pain from the angle of purchase
Pain from the angle of exhaustion
Pain from the angle of duty
Pain from the angle of doing your chores
Pain from the angle of getting off sexually
Pain from the angle of investment
Pain from the angle of policy
Pain from the angle of self-mythology
Pain from the angle of housing as commodity
Pain from the angle of medical malpractice
Pain from the angle of memory
Pain from the angle of infection
Pain from the angle of necessary revolution

Disposability Blues

Now & then I say to someone:
    "What you did hurt me
      You hurt me, & that's real
      Please don't do that   please"

& they say:
    "Avery what the fuck
      You're not making any sense right now
      I'm scared   you're being really scary
      Stay away from me"

It's the repetition   the dull object
of tgirl trauma

We ask too much
Scary girls with hairy hearts

Oh well   another loss is another loss is another loss is another loss is
another loss

Bruise (v.): to continue through the river, even as He grows heavier

We're not okay. November was meant to be over by now. A day is so long
and sweet when I know what your tools are for. Can you imagine walking
for forty years in the desert your God gave you. We're not okay. Because
your God is merciful she almost feeds you enough. For months it seemed
I was all you had. Packets of food shotgun down from heaven and crater the
sand and one of them hits your sister in the eye and then your sister is blind
in one eye. Why be someone when I can't be the fuel you need. In March
the sky was purple all day. It didn't make sense. It just was. The world is like
that sometimes. You settle into suffering like a worn-down chair. People fuck
and get evicted and raped and lose jobs and take worse jobs and stumble
but keep walking and float cleanly into the sky, in the desert your God gave
you. August and September are plotting together like rats. I fold myself into
usefulness. The God of love plants a pillar of fire in the sky so you don't have
to sleep at night. We're still not okay. I used to think I should bend my body
into a bridge, for you. I used to think this all the time.

Family / History

1.

You're not dead if I remember you hurting me.

I hope summer breaks your back.

You drape your voice around the house.

I sit in the swelter, reading, rocking.

You say, "Don't, it might bring the house down."

2.

The still-living river flooded my grandmother's basement.
We painted the floors and walls a blaring white.

Told myself kneeling, "Poetry is stupid and selfish.
I write when I want to look like I'm using my hands."

Forget the words, not the teeth, wet and deflating.
In this house we are our function.

Inheritance law as expressed by meat.
Kneeling to paint, to flatten.

A family's murderous disconnect.
Power is successive, like water, or paving over water.

I gouge myself from the world.
Detachment and profit as the only white memory.

The river, breathing, pooled on the carpet despite us.
We painted our house so it hurt the eyes.

On my knees I know what my parents are.
I can see where *the* body becomes *a* body.

3.

A house is a slim wall against the storm.

Oh summer so sickly.

I'm crawling back to the language again.

Oh amygdala.

It's oozing in, thru the floor & the ceiling.

Oh the poems are scabbing.

A bedroom is a slim wall against a family.

Your father won't clean up the mess.

You left your shame in the living room.

Like a storm, but like the rain, only gentle, like dripping water.

Oh the names I could tell.

A house is a slim wall dripping blood.

Oh in Montreal they're cool.

A door is a penetrable thing.

We burned the old city down.

Oh old man is big oh new man loves old man.

Oh old man is bad oh new man hates old man.

Oh old man is gone oh new man is big.

Oh let the blood guide you.

Oh I'm losing you again.

Oh here it comes, up through my insides – but gently, in droplets.

4.

When my grandmother dies, I'll cough up coal.
I'll hate myself for having blocked her number.
She said this would happen. "I'm getting old,
it's not as though I'll be around forever."

I'll lie down all day, eating guilt and rot.
Hide at the funeral like a mob boss,
back to the wall, expecting a gunshot.
Christ, what a heavy, jagged thing I lost.

When she dies, I'll walk into the river.
Stand in the current a while, the freezing
flailing waves against me. I will give her
my body, bloodless, beaten, and heaving.

It'd be nice to shake for a reason that's not
my body remembering things I forgot.

Act II: The Other

On Shame

Can you forgive me
for how you hurt me so bad

Night at the Sexual Assault Centre Art Show

Out of place immediately.
Scan artwork for clues. *ale body the female body the*
female body.   Get punch.
Notice plastic cup shards emerging through your
fingers like stalagmites. *it break, of course they do,*
that break.
Sink through the space like mud. *nel.*

Card saying it wasn't your fault. Room full of faces
lurching like a trash compactor.
Packing paper on the wall says write whose fault it
really was. *A signup sheet.*
Stare at it like a dryer full of sneakers:
shaking, mostly empty, clattering.
Female body the female space into which the male
Surprise a girl as she leaves the bathroom and sees
you waiting. *eyes she knows what you are.*
Wash your face. Remember after.
                    You scrubbed skin off your filth.
See reflected offscreen someone talking about the
phallus.
Horror in how you spill dip.
Believe you will puke. *ember this.*
Sit in ways that hurt your legs. *is.*
Wish your body could shrink.

34

Intruder the place immediately.

Scan artwork The female body the female body the
female body.   *Get punch.*

Notice plastic cup shards emerging through your
fingers like s Hands that break, of course they do,
that break.

Careening blocking view like shrapnel.

Card saying it wasn't your fault. Biarm This of *faces*
lurching like a trash compactor.
Packing paper on the wall says write whose fault it
really was. A signup sheet.
Stare at it like a dryer full of sneakers:
shaking, mostly empty, clattering.
Female body the female space into which the male
sinks, disguised in overlarge sweater, invading.
Terror in her eyes she knows what you are.
Wash your face. Remember after.

          You scrubbed skin off your filth.

See reflected offscreen someone talking about the
phallus.
Horror in how you spill dip.
Your shoulders will remember this.
Your shoulders will remember this.
Wish your body could shrink.

Reasons Not to Get Married

Money

Unstuck in time

Your parents did it

Your parents didn't do it

Nudity

Impending apocalypse

Unshakeable sense of impending apocalypse

Can't find your special fucking handkerchief

Exhaustion

A Pearl

When we fucked
the old old fears fell on my fingers

Left to the bathroom & I was ruined
by small white moths on the kitchen floor

We'd left the window open
I saw them all at once

I knew you had that phobia
so I killed them
their wings made little *krak* sounds as I crushed them
Each one made that little *krak* sound

It felt so gentle
We broke up that weekend

I want to hide that gentleness
A pearl for me, alone
But want to write it

I'm a vampire that way
One of the wounds I'll have to gape
is breaking small white moths under soft white tissue

Reposition I: Burn Something

Burn something. Relief rots into your chest. Believe in the insistent symbolism of fire. Three weeks later, or two, burn again. A book. Hair. Anything that smells like your abuser. Burn everything you need to, every time you need to. Find new and creative venues at which to burn things. Taunt the authorities. Develop rituals. Involve salt, knives, old TVs. Burn through bibles like a rogue inquisitor. Grow new names. Strike poses. Spit on burning things. Piss on burning things. You're not the good guy here. Hoard your abuser's belongings for fuel. Don't do anything as stupid as move on. Turn off your smoke alarm. Scare your neighbour and feel a flood of comfort. Grow your anger like a painful plant. Be the small-minded petty tyrant you want to see in the world. If you slow down, you wilt into blunt, abject self-knowledge. Keep your eye on the prize. The night is long. Slithering, chattering things wait in the dark.

Reposition II: WHAT MASK

The memories want fuel. The guts want meat.
I am an abuser to this slice of toast.
This is the forbidden face. I am smiling with teeth.

I keep my neglect surgical and neat.
This toast will relearn what it feels like to rot.
The memories want fuel. The guts want meat.

I bloat ragged with power. My skin is tight.
My body holds force like a sewer in a flood.
This is the forbidden face. I am smiling with teeth.

Maggots and predators ooze in the heat.
Bury this toast in a bag like a pet I never loved.
The memories want fuel. The guts want meat.

Skin gurgles and roils with power beneath.
I'm not just a girl anymore. I am a host.
This is the forbidden face. I am smiling with teeth.

I am whole and transformed and fucked clean and white.
I almost held you, you were almost good, almost.
The memories want fuel. The guts want meat.
This is the forbidden face. I am smiling with teeth.

the purest breakup poem is the bit in *the lighthouse*
when robert pattinson makes willem dafoe his pup & then
immediately kills him & then Dies

like falling & swooping, *you're such a pretty thing.*
the scum begs lower. i build a reason, & then lose it.
what a generous knife.

aren't we having fun?
what else are you for?

is it freeing to be forgotten?
there's anger in dingy desire,
& then there's wilting without you.

i know that look. don't try shit.
half the time, *i love* i want to fuck someone
to prove i'm not *pliable.*
fucking you anymore.

the other half, i want a bird to peck the idea of sex
out of me.

we'd made a cookbook together. a promise, a future
in bone broth.
oh, but that's not fair – it's not that he lied, it's that
he didn't know. *this poem is direct & linear. that's*
why it's about dick.

like falling & swooping, you're such a pretty thing.
the scum begs lower. *i build a reason, & then lose it.*
what a generous knife.

aren't we having fun?
what else are you for?

is it freeing to be forgotten?
there's anger in dingy desire,
& then there's wilting without you.

i know that look. don't try shit.
half the time, i love when you're *i want to wreck someone*
to prove i'm not pliable.
fucking scary & sacred. smirking & salient.

the other half, i want a bird to peck the idea of sex
out of me.

we'd made a cookbook together. a promise, a future
in bone broth.
oh, but that's not fair – it's not that he lied, it's that
he didn't know. this poem is direct & linear. that's
why it's about dick.

41

Greenhouse

You carry quiet thunder with you. What splendour,
how grand. You can still take this from me. *bring me to you.*
You can still take anything from me by appearing in
the hallway like thunder, silent, clasping a sweater,
devouring.

Without hands in the greenhouse the reading washes *falling washes*
over me. *back over me.*

What violence, what romance.
Close together among the plants, unmoving. We are
too packed to move. *again and I can't move.*

Of course you wouldn't ask. Of course you'd text me
to say you're excited *it gut-rot. You sat in the front*
row.
A loss of touch
A loss of blood *on in the skin. The heart rate slows,*
a visit behind glass, a tunnel. From far away I hear
From far away you reach out and your hand is on *the hanging plants.*
me again.

42

You carry quiet thunder with you. What splendour,
*how grand. You can sti*I keep losing things* to you.*
You can still take anything from me by appearing in
the hallway like thunder, silent, clasping a sweater,
devouring.

*Without hands in the greenhouse t*Without blood*es*
you are *back over me.*

What violence, what romance.
Close together among the plants, unmoving. We are
You are close to me again and I can't move.

Of course you wouldn't ask. Of course you'd text me
I got your text and felt gut-rot. You sat in the front
row.
A loss of touch
A loss of sensation in the skin. The heart rate slows,
a visit behind glass, a tunnel. From far away I hear
the reader describing the attack, between the people,
among the hanging plants.

Sonnet Under Ice

I had a poem in his magazine.
They paid me fifty dollars. That's my price.
She told us what she did. It had a sheen,
a beauty like a body under ice.

They let him teach again, the fucking cowards.
My poem wasn't even any good.
I guess we all forgot who he devoured
cuz it was easy. He asked me who I'd

fuck. So punctured people punctured people.
We learned about how conflict's not abuse.
We have to work with her. It's just carceral
logic to protect the girls she raped.

What the fuck is rape supposed to rhyme with.
Art is bootlicking. Run fast. Trust no bitch.

Act III: The Relations of Production

Pop Quiz

1. what is healing
   a. what is healin g
   b. what i   s healing
                                        c. what is healing what is
healing

2. what is healing
                                  a. what is hea   ling
             b. what is healing
3. what is healing

4. what   is healing   what is healing   what is healing   wh
   at is healing
                   a. what is healing
                                b. what is healing what is healing what
                                   is

5. heali   ng what is healing
        a. what is healing what is healing   what is healingwhat is healing

6. what is healing whatis
        a. healing what is healing what is healing what is healing what is heal
           ing

7. what is healing

    a. what is healing   what is healing what is healing
        what i s healing   what is healing what is healing what is healing
        what is healing what is healing what is   healing
        what is healing what   is healingwhatishealingwhatishe
                         b. aling what is he aling what is he
                            aling what is he aling what is he
                            aling what is he aling what is he
                            aling what is he alingwhatishealing

8. what i she aling what i she aling what i she aling what i she aling what i
    she aling what i she alingwhatishealingwhatis
healingwhatishealingwhatishealingwhatishealingwhatishealingwhatis
healingwhatishealingwhatishealingwhatishealingwhatishealingwhatis
healingwhatishealingwhatishealingwhatishealingwhatishealingwhatis
healingwhatishealingwhatishealingwhatishealingwhatishealingwhatis
healingwhatiswhatishealingwhatishealingwhatishealingwhatishealing
whatishealingwhatishealingwhatis

Color Study: Unemployed

I wanted green/ city bus yanking/ Fell into gutshot doctor/ distrust & back pain/ reader, you don't get the details/ I wanted green/ I got disallowed back pay/ I was dry & dragging/ black sky through plexiglass/ the trip home can swallow you/ I wanted green/ I got lost in the metro/ winter fell like an axe/ disjoint & shrapnel/ I walked home & slipped/ night at 4pm like a maw/ I wanted green/ I saw months & months stretched out like a corpse/ I wanted green/ I wanted green/ I wanted green/ I wanted green

Color Study: Desk v. Window

Poems wanna be like women singing –
voices strained, rough & gasping

You're men, all of you
You're men, all of you
You're men, all of you
You're men, all of you

I want a rusted woman
I want a curt, caught breath
I want a hand in brown hair
I want a burned-out tree –
callous, brittle, standing, bound

49

Sonnet for the Boss's Son

His high school energy is off the charts.
He speaks like he's been told to clean his plate
before he can play FIFA. In his heart,
he's in a constant spiritual state

of publicly applying Axe Body Spray.
He swears at his mom when she gives him work.
(She's the CEO.) In meetings he plays
YouTube videos, his phone behind a book.

He's never acknowledged my existence.
In my internal ranking of co-workers
based on how likely, given the chance,
they'd be to hate-crime me, he's a rising star.

He's a cardboard cut-out of a rich kid,
a vacuous whirlwind of cash and id.

Color Study: Full-Time

I wanted blue. I struggle with the shape of my new life. Trees here look
like knives peeling back the sky. I work forty-three hours a week and I'm
not in love anymore. My new life suplexes me. Sometimes the bus is late.
Sometimes the exits freeze over. When I try to jerk off, I think of my ex,
and have to stop. Change is measured in hourly wage and solitude. Some-
times you probe the wound. I wanted blue. The CEO quotes Tom Cruise.
Her children joke about cutting people's pay. We all smile and laugh.
I wanted a riverbed rest, blue and barren. Sometimes the rich sound like
puppies. I wanted blue. I'm never alone, at work, but I am lonely. I wanted
blue. Sometimes I thought I'd find it.

Color Study: Crying@Work

slipping from call to call,   *i wanted it*
crackling & automated   *drained out*
                                     i wanted red

hi, i'm avery, calling from ipsos – we're doing some
research on public opinion,
would you like to –   *bleeding block of a bed*
                           flashback drag-over
                           i wanted it

"get a real job!" the guy yells *drag girl fleshbag*
pours his hateful head *my colors bled* into the phone
i wanted red

slipping into memory like a tar pit   *hanging plants*
living things, dripping bubbling muck of knowing
i wanted it

her colors filling me what happened isn't over
hissing livid thing   i want what i don't
red want rot hands

empty boy she's in the room *leaks by* i'm in
i'm in the *rent rot* room i'm always in – *residue*
i wanted red stained, skin hissing,
i wanted it trapped in a bed big & colorless

i lurch at my desk while the hanging plants watch

slipping from call to call,   i wanted it

crackling & automated   drained out

                 i wanted red

hi, i'm avery, calling from ipsos – we're doing some

research on public opinion,

would you like to –   bleeding block of a bed

                 flashback drag-over

                 i wanted it

"get a real job!" the guy yells drag girl fleshbag

pours his hateful head my colors bled out *into* the phone

i wanted red

slipping into memory like a tar pit   hanging plants

living things, dripping out *bubbling muck of knowing*

i wanted it

her colors filling me *what happened isn't over*

hissing livid thing   *i want what i don't*

red want rot hands

empty boy *she's in the room* leaks by *i'm in*

i'm in the rent rot *room i'm always in –* residue

i wanted red *stained, skin hissing,*

i wanted it *trapped in a bed big & colorless*

i lurch at my desk while the hanging plants watch

Suicide in Translation

1.

Life is hell & gets worse.

Unsteady, desperate, hateful.

Life is something that happens to you.

Sex is something that happens to you.

You're scared to write it down

or leave your room. You don't want anyone

to find your body.

When they do, they jerk off.

2.

Life buries you, then buries you.

It begs to bruise you again.

Life writes you down, pushing you deeper.

You don't want anyone to have to love you,

touch you.

You stay in your room.

3.

You're in the pit. You sink deeper.

The pit shakes.

The pit happens to you.

You try to fuck it.

Writing it is self-harm.

Your breath got caught when they took off your pants

to find your body.

You stay in your room.

4.

Life sinks into you, lubed & desperate.

You shake, like you did last time.

It's the same story –

it happens to you, it happens to you, it happens to you.

You offer sex like it'll stop the cave-in.

You crawl deeper into your pit, hateful,

so they can't find your body.

You want to fossilize, dreamless,

in the hole at the end of the game,

& stay there.

5.

In 2004,

5800 feet underground,

two men were trapped.

They were unable to climb.

They crawled 300 feet

through a narrow, knife-sharp tunnel,

descending.

They called it *the way to the dream.*

The cave flooded.

Their scuba gear hadn't fit through the dream.

The cave happened to them.

They found the deepest point a human had.

They called it *game over,* and stayed there.

How to Live Alone

Move slowly – mind the cramps

Dip into memories like a too-hot bath

Find a meal you swear by

Unpack, then stop unpacking

Get a crush on someone in another country

Grow a love-hate relationship with "tasks"

Close your eyes – when that doesn't help, pass out

As cringe as it is, get into yoga

Adopt a cat

See your ex on Tinder – worse, on Lex

See your friends on the front balcony

See abuse on the windowsill

See eviction on your phone screen

See threats where they are and where they aren't

See tearing seams in your friends' shoulders

See life as subsidiary to the notion of "small businesses"

See death in handy little charts and graphs

Wake up when your cat walks onto your chest, then fall back asleep,
    grateful for a weight that's not your own

Houses and People

Let's get one thing straight
Just because this city knows my secrets doesn't mean you get to
These are for who they're for

Downtown – to B.
I learned to be touched
in that tiny dorm room

NDG – to B.
I held your trust like a bowl of soup
in my parents' basement

Mile End – to B.
Every time I pass I think, there's your old apartment
But I can't recognize it anymore

West Island – to K.
Remember those two ancient cats?
Watching us, trusting each other

Côte-des-Neiges – to G.
It was a cheap place with amber evenings
And of course we both lost it

St-Henri – to S.

Ice skittering across the kitchen

Joy on the dirty floor

Parc Ex – to M.

You held my trust like a sick animal

in that ghost of a good life

Outremont – to M.

Neko Case song in the kitchen

I thanked you – what a year, what a year, what a year

Verdun – to myself

Walked past that old apartment

It's a sleek appalling condo now

I leave my early 20s and realize –

I was the bad ex too

Grief Sestina

Again I can't stand in the shower.
I hate how much I miss you.
Careening in & out of memory,
stubbing my toe, sending things flying – it was like this all year,
March's shadow tall & burning.
Loss after loss

after loss after loss.
Collapsing in the shower,
violins screeching – but no killer, just you, burning
a floodlight hole in my back. You
carve an old calendar. You cut away the years.
I want to think I honored your memory,

but of course I didn't. Your memory
is brittle bugs. Every loss
is the same – all the bad years
line up one by one. You shower
every day, don't you?
Doesn't matter if the water's burning.

Used to wake up drunk on dreams of suicide, burning
with the bastard hope that my memory
would breeze past you.
Didn't want a leaky death – to leave loss

behind like puke in the metro. Oh, to evaporate in the shower!
This was 2015 or so. One long horrible year

just like every other year.
Time as a dim candle – spent but still burning –
one long cascade – grief as a constant shower
of spiny, jerky muscle memory.
A blunt, ugly rhythm of loss.
The one thing shared by every you

is how it's so fast & so slow – you
disappear overnight & that night becomes a year.
Wanna hear a bad joke? It's loss,
same as the last five times! A trash fire burning
in spits & sputters. You can't make a mouth from a memory,
but you try, & it brings you crashing down in the shower.

When you wither in loss, you're
a plant over-showered for years –
roots gasping, lungs burning. You leak memory, you lose leaves.

Bruise (n.): an inability to sleep

The Leader, he cleans my hair with his feet. Abuse is everywhere. I know your name, then forget it. Remember the heat in Brooklyn, the word for it was *groping*. Sobbing in the dive bar. Sometimes close to knowing, but it tilts and sinks. New York is too many bodies close together. Our work is so important, he lied. Have you ever kicked the wall of a bathroom in a dive bar, twice, hard. There are three abusers in this poem. There is abuse everywhere. Everyone is hurting and everyone is fucking and in a different bathroom I counted down from a hundred, slowly. I'm told that 80s dykes hurt each other because it was the only language they had. I'm told I'm mistaken. He teaches at Concordia, you know, do you know. I know his name: three ugly consonants. My friend had a patch that said "avoid gossip" and I thought never, how else do you save lives. East Village houses are bursting and blushing. No, it was more than three abusers. No, less. I forget who's been hurt or how. They held my hair like a throat, and I've never met him even though he teaches at Concordia, and he let me crash at his place the last night before I left Brooklyn. Does it get confusing, how it all becomes the same? Pain that resists discreteness and begs for discreetness. Don't you wish you knew their names. When the Leader plants his feet in your hair, I promise you will feel clean.

Color Study: Horrible Dance

wanna stop writing in past tense

wanna shape God

wanna keep

a rhythm going, wanna – it's

happening – keep moving,

wanna know you

again – it's

happening – wanna be

kept, wanna be,

just wanna be –

it's happening – trees

walk around at night,

wanna know, did you know me,

did you know me,

did i live in your memory,

will i live in a

pandemic without a job,

in a room alone –

it's happening now, you know.

i rose to meet you with red hands –

"thank you," you said – "fuck you," i said –

we were both talking to me

my process is easy – this is an apology –

this is not an apology –

it comes to me –

i see my rapist – i go looking –

am i sure violence –

is unromantic?

wanna find that ex

at some punk show – did you share the gofundme? – and grind

his skull into concrete

what an uneven life you can live – we're keeping tabs

 – her friend killed herself –

uneven life you can live

with surprises & loving mammals

while still the person who raped me –

i think they're in the hospital again?

suicide attempt but a – you'd kill me

if you thought it'd save my life – half-assed one –

what an ugly way to live – link

your paypal? ignore the name –

wanna – it felt so good

to do what you wanted – find the guy

who raped my friend

& insert a crowbar & lever

his kneecaps open –

you didn't hear?

they died

no, a new one,

that was last month –

each new time,

my body remembers a crueller you –

i shouldn't publish – you could see it
– you'd be so hurt –
what do you get from this?
are you happy you're reading this?
it's happening, spinning
faster – red pours out
my eyes – Aren't You
Glad You Came To See The Dance? –
ripjaw buddy-buddy,
you're in it now,
it's happening, now,
my hands around your throat &
my wings spread high –
do you remember me now?
do you remember me now?
do you remember me now?

I want lavender, maybe,
or something deeper.
Hulking machines,
dead underground.
Bodies blooming, some deep color
or other.

Good Advice from an Undiscovered Atom

Whirl through life
at great speed. Find people you love
and try to collide with them.

Shout even if most people
are sure you are invisible. See gravity
for what it is. Do not forget to spin.

Make sure if people try to break you open
to explode with violent force.
Be the smallest of your kind, and maybe
the strongest.

Notes

The poems which appear as scores for two overlapping voices, with
faded underlying text, have lifted the technique from Robert Bringhurst's *The Blue
Roofs of Japan* (William Hoffer, 1986), as introduced to me by Katherine McLeod.

On Womanhood

"I get older, they stay the same age" is an infamous line from Matthew
McConaughey in Richard Linklater's *Dazed and Confused*. The "Empire affair"
refers to Janice Raymond's *The Transsexual Empire: The Making of the She-Male*
(Beacon Press, 1979), which infamously argues that transsexuals should be
"morally mandated out of existence" and includes extensive personal attacks
on Sandy Stone; as well as to Stone's 1987 essay "The Empire Strikes Back: A
Posttranssexual Manifesto." N.b. that Stone has implied that Raymond's work on
The Transsexual Empire coincided neatly with the alleged girlfriend-stealing.

The Schopenhauer quote is from his 1851 essay "On Women."

"Epaulets" is referring to something stupid Eileen Myles said in an interview once that
trans women on Twitter spent a while riffing on. The Weather Girls reference is to
the song "It's Raining Men." Julia Serano's dualist theory of transmisogyny – in which
trans women are perceived either as hypersexual, perfectly passing, "traps" with huge
schlongs; or as failed half-men, unconvincing in our grasps at femininity, most potently
through the image of bottom surgery as an embarrassing, emasculating wound – is
drawn most from her book *Whipping Girl* (Seal Press, 2007). The mtf transgender
resource website Susan's Place, most popular in the 90s/2000s, is known for its header
reading "We Stand at the Crossroads of Gender, Balanced on the Sharp Edge of a
Knife." If you're reading this book, you should probably read Leslie Feinberg's *Stone
Butch Blues* (Firebrand Books, 1993) if you haven't already.

Family/History

Many lines from the third section are lifted verbatim from dialogue in FromSoftware's *Bloodborne*.

Reasons Not to Get Married

The "special fucking handkerchief" is an *Othello* joke.

A Pearl

This poem is titled after the Mitski song of the same name, off her 2018 album *Be the Cowboy*.

Reposition II: WHAT MASK

"WHAT MASK" is a track off Kyle Reimergartin's 2013 album *F J O R D S*, accompanying his experimental game of the same name.

the purest breakup poem is the bit in *the lighthouse* when robert pattinson makes willem dafoe his pup & then immediately kills him & then Dies

The obvious reference is to Robert Eggers' 2019 film *The Lighthouse*. The less obvious one is to "falling & swooping," a refrain in Jeff VanderMeer's *Southern Reach* trilogy.

Sonnet Under Ice

This poem's title comes from Violet Gehringer. *Conflict Is Not Abuse* (Arsenal Pulp Press, 2016) is a much-discoursed book by Sarah Schulman. "Trust no bitch" is a line from, regrettably, *Orange Is the New Black*.

Color Studies

The motif of wanting a color, present in each Color Study, is riffing off "a poem should show not tell" by jos charles, from their 2016 book *safe space* (Ahsahta Press, 2016). That poem ends with "I wanted red/ I wanted red/ I wanted red/ I wanted red."

Suicide in Translation

The horrible spelunking expedition referenced was introduced to me, and is wonderfully elaborated on, in Jacob Geller's YouTube video "Fear of Depths."

Grief Sestina

The "violins screeching – but no killer" is riffing off the shower scene in Alfred Hitchcock's *Psycho* (1960).

Bruise (n.): an inability to sleep

"The Leader, he cleans my hair with his feet" is the closing line of a poem from *Dear Leader* (Coach House Press, 2015) by Damian Rogers, introduced to me by Sina Queyras.

Color Study: Horrible Dance

The idea of "shaping God" plays a major part in Octavia Butler's *Parable of the Sower* (Four Walls Eight Windows, 1993).

Good Advice from an Undiscovered Atom

This poem is riffing off "Postcard from the Moon" by Brett Elizabeth Jenkins, introduced to me by Matthew Ogle's "Pome" service.

Acknowledgments

To everyone who helped sculpt the book – Eli, Ev, River, Rex, Adam, Sina, all the rest.

To Emily, Ev, & Rain, for being the backbone of me being able to start this thing. To everyone who let me yell to them while writing.

To the commie book club – I apologize for not making it more dialectically insufferable.

To Is, for the guidance.

To Gab.

To everyone I'm forgetting to thank by virtue of wrangling an unruly memory on a deadline.

To everyone at all the housing orgs around Montreal.

To trans women. To trans women!

To everyone with whom I've shared a heart.

Avery Lake is a worker and writer living in occupied Tiohtià:ke. She attended Concordia University and is not in the scene.